The Biography of Vanilla

Julie Karner

 Crabtree Publishing Company
www.crabtreebooks.com

Crabtree Publishing Company
www.crabtreebooks.com

For Huck
1968 - 2006

Coordinating editor: Ellen Rodger
Series editor: Carrie Gleason
Project editor: L. Michelle Nielsen
Editors: Rachel Eagen, Adrianna Morganelli
Production coordinator: Rosie Gowsell
Production assistance: Samara Parent
Art direction: Rob MacGregor
Scanning technician: Arlene Arch-Wilson
Photo research: Allison Napier

Consultant: Patricia Rain, Author of *Vanilla: The Cultural History of the World's Favorite Flavor and Fragrance* and, President of the Vanilla.COMpany (www.vanilla.com); Vanilla plant legend (p. 8) courtesy of Patricia Rain

Photo Credits: Melba Photo Agency/Alamy: p. 19 (top); Biblioteca Medicea-Laurenziana, Florence, Italy/The Bridgeman Art Library International: p. 9 (bottom); Palacio Nacional, Mexico City, Mexico, Giraudon/The Bridgeman Art Library: p. 4; Private Collection, Bonhams, London, UK/The Bridgeman Art Library International: p. 5 (bottom); Private Collection, Peter Newark American Pictures/The Bridgeman Art Library International: p. 17; Morton Beebe/Corbis: p. 25 (bottom); Bettmann/Corbis: p. 26 (bottom); Cuartoscuro/Corbis Sygma: p. 30 (bottom); Reinhard Eisele/Corbis: p. 21(bottom); Owen Franken/Corbis: p. 25 (top); Peter Guttman/Corbis: p. 19 (bottom); Hal Horwitz/Corbis: p. 26 (top); Silva Joao/Corbis Sygma: p. 18, p. 23, p. 31; John R. Jones; Papilio/Corbis: p. 21 (top); Lake County Museum/Corbis: p. 27;

Michael Maslan Historic Photographs /Corbis: p. 24; Flavio Pagani/Sygma/Corbis: p. 5 (top); Tim Page/Corbis: cover; photocuisine/Corbis: p. 29 (top right); Kevin Schafer/Corbis: p. 13 (top); Hubert Stadler/Corbis: p. 14; Swim Ink 2, LLC/Corbis: p. 7 (bottom); Graham West /zefa/Corbis: p. 9 (top), p. 12 (bottom top left); George Marks/Retrofile/Getty Images: p. 29 (bottom right); The Granger Collection, New York: p. 12 (top), p. 13 (bottom); The Board of Trustees of the Armouries/Heritage-Images/The Image Works: p. 12 (bottom right); Mary Evans Picture Library/The Image Works: p. 15; S. Murphy-Larronde/Index Stock: p. 22; Kevin O'Hara/Index Stock Imagery: p. 20; North Wind/North Wind Picture Archives: p. 10 (bottom), p. 11; Peter Barker/Panos Pictures: p. 1; Sheila Terry/Photo Researchers, Inc.: p. 8; Other images from stock CDs.

Illustration: Rob MacGregor: p. 16

Cartography: Jim Chernishenko: p. 6

Cover: The flavor of vanilla is enjoyed all over the world. Many of the top vanilla growing countries border or are islands in the Indian Ocean, including Madagascar, Comoros, India, and Indonesia.

Title page: Each vanilla bean is checked and then sorted into a group based on its quality.

Contents: Vanilla is the most popular flavor of ice cream.

Library and Archives Canada Cataloguing in Publication

Karner, Julie, 1976-
    The biography of vanilla / Julie Karner.

(How did that get here?)
Includes index.
ISBN-13: 978-0-7787-2490-2 (bound)
ISBN-10: 0-7787-2490-5 (bound)
ISBN-13: 978-0-7787-2526-8 (pbk.)
ISBN-10: 0-7787-2526-X (pbk.)

    1. Vanilla--Juvenile literature. I. Title. II. Series.

SB307.V2K37 2006   j633.8'2   C2006-902469-3

Library of Congress Cataloging-in-Publication Data

Karner, Julie, 1976-
    The biography of vanilla / written by Julie Karner.
      p. cm. -- (How did that get here?)
    Includes index.
    ISBN-13: 978-0-7787-2490-2 (rlb)
    ISBN-10: 0-7787-2490-5 (rlb)
    ISBN-13: 978-0-7787-2526-8 (pb)
    ISBN-10: 0-7787-2526-X (pb)
    1. Vanilla--Juvenile literature. I. Title. II. Series.
    SB307.V2K37 2006
    633.8'2--dc22

    2006014374

Crabtree Publishing Company

Published in Canada
Crabtree Publishing
616 Welland Ave.
St. Catharines, ON
L2M 5V6

Published in the United States
Crabtree Publishing
PMB16A
350 Fifth Ave., Suite 3308
New York, NY 10118

Published in the United Kingdom
Crabtree Publishing
White Cross Mills
High Town, Lancaster
LA1 4XS

Published in Australia
Crabtree Publishing
386 Mt. Alexander Rd.
Ascot Vale (Melbourne)
VIC 3032

Contents

What is Vanilla?

Vanilla is a spice that is valued for its flavor and aroma. Spices are parts of plants, such as the leaves, or fruits, that have been dried. They are used to add scent and flavor to products. The taste of vanilla beans can be found in many drinks and foods, such as soft drinks, cookies, cakes, and chocolate treats. The flavor is also used to mask unpleasant tastes in medicines and cigarettes, while the scent of vanilla is found in perfumes, soaps, and candles.

The Aztec people, who lived in present-day Mexico, were among the first to use vanilla. They traded for vanilla with other peoples, such as the Totonac, who also lived in Mexico.

The Vanilla Bean

Vanilla beans are the seed pods, or fruit, of vanilla orchids, which are flowering vines that grow in the **tropics**. The vines grow to lengths of 50 feet (15 meters) or more, and cling to trees, bushes, or posts for support. The flower and the immature, or young, bean do not have a distinct scent. The familiar vanilla fragrance develops only after the bean has ripened and **fermented**. During fermentation, the **chemical compounds** in beans break down and form new compounds. There are more than 500 chemical compounds found in vanilla beans, including vanillin, which is the main source of the rich flavor and aroma of vanilla.

A Pricey Spice

Vanilla is one of the most expensive spices to buy. The high price is due to the amount of time and work needed to grow and **cure** vanilla. It takes up to five years from the time a vine is planted until the beans are ready to be sold. The people who farm vanilla and prepare it for sale must be experts on the spice. They must know the best time to harvest, or pick, the beans so that they will be of top quality and bring in the best prices. Today, vanilla is grown mostly in **developing countries** and is sold mainly to people in western, or developed, countries. The United States buys more vanilla than any other country in the world.

▲ Vanilla is a commodity, or a good that is traded around the world.

Love Potion?

Scent is a powerful sense. Many people believe smells can alter moods and evoke memories. Over 4,000 years ago, the ancient Egyptians were among the first to use scent in the form of **incense** and perfumes. Today, the perfume industry makes billions of dollars every year, with many of the most popular scents using vanilla as an ingredient. Scientists have discovered that the scent of vanilla can calm a person's nerves and reduce stress. The Aztec people of Mexico believed vanilla could help people fall in love.

◀ Today, real and artificial, or manufactured, vanilla are used in many perfumes.

Vanilla Lands

Vanilla crops grow only in the warm, wet regions of the tropics. The tropics is an area directly north and south of the equator. Most tropical regions are warm all year, which is ideal for growing vanilla since the vines need temperatures that average between 70° Fahrenheit and 90° Fahrenheit (21° Celsius and 32° Celsius). Vanilla vines also need about 100 inches (254 centimeters) of rain to grow and develop. While rain is necessary, a dry period of about two months is also needed for the vines to flower and produce fruit, or beans. Heavy rains during this time would wash the flowers off of the vines before they could be **pollinated**.

An Orchid with Flavor

The vanilla plant is a member of *Orchidaceae*, or the orchid family, which is the largest family of flowering plants. Vanilla is the only orchid that has fruit that can be eaten. There are at least 150 species, or types, of vanilla vine, but only two are used to make vanilla products, such as **extracts**. *Vanilla planifolia*, the more common of the two, is grown in many places, including Mexico, Madagascar, and Indonesia. *Vanilla tahitensis* is grown almost exclusively in Tahiti and Papua New Guinea. All of the vanilla grown today can be traced to the wild vanilla vines of Mexico and Central America.

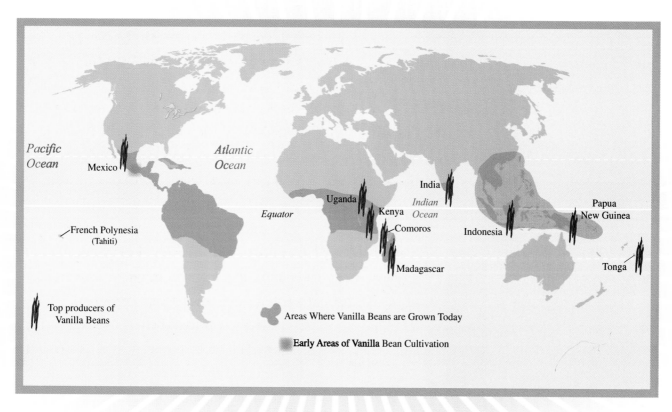

The climate and soil that vanilla vines are grown in affect the beans. The flavor and aroma of a vanilla vine grown in one region is different than the same type of vine grown in another region.

Around the World

In the 1500s, Spanish **conquistadors** who were exploring lands in present-day Mexico met **Mesoamerican** peoples who used vanilla to flavor foods and drinks. The conquistadors brought the bean back to Spain. Vanilla was used to flavor a chocolate drink that combined **cacao beans**, vanilla, corn, water, and honey. The drink spread from Spain to France, England, and the rest of Europe during the early 1600s. In the late 1700s, vanilla made its way to the United States, where it became the flavor of choice for a new treat, ice cream. Today, vanilla is still the most popular ice cream flavor.

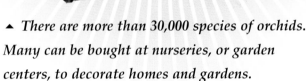

▲ *There are more than 30,000 species of orchids. Many can be bought at nurseries, or garden centers, to decorate homes and gardens.*

Supply and Demand

The price of vanilla is constantly changing. It depends on how much vanilla is available and how many people or companies want to buy it. If vanilla is in high demand, or many people want to buy it, prices tend to be high, and if there is not enough vanilla available because storms destroyed one season's crops, then prices rise even further. Prices decrease if there is a surplus, or more vanilla available for sale than is wanted by the public. Traders and curers then offer lower prices to farmers, which farmers must accept because selling the beans at a low price is better than not selling them at all. Vanilla farmers rely on this money to support their families.

"Isn't it nice Grandma?"

VANILLA CHOCOLATE (PINK WRAPPER)

Candy makers were using vanilla by the late 1800s. This advertisement is for vanilla flavored chocolate.

7

Ancient Vanilla

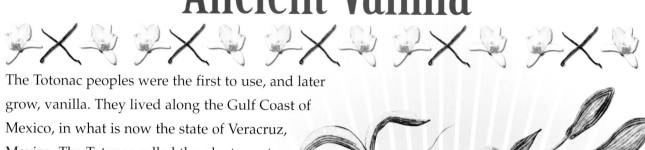

The Totonac peoples were the first to use, and later grow, vanilla. They lived along the Gulf Coast of Mexico, in what is now the state of Veracruz, Mexico. The Totonac called the plant *xanat* (pronounced CHA-nat), and believed in a legend that told of the first vanilla plant springing from the souls of a prince and princess.

The Totonac Legend of Xanat

In the city of Papantla, Mexico, a very beautiful girl was born to King Tenitzli and his wife. They named their daughter Princess Tzacopontziza, or "Morning Star." Morning Star's life was dedicated, or given, to the goddess Tonacayohua, and she was forbidden to marry. One day, while the princess was gathering flowers, she was spotted by Prince Zkatan-Oxga, or "Young Deer." They fell in love and decided to run off together but they were soon discovered. As punishment, Morning Star and Young Deer were beheaded. Where their blood soaked into the ground, a bush soon began to grow. A vine grew up among its branches , and produced a small, pale orchid. When the fruit of the orchid ripened and burst open, it released a beautiful fragrance. The souls of the prince and princess had transformed into the bush and vanilla orchid.

Totonac peoples offered vanilla as a gift to the gods, so the gods would keep them safe.

The First Uses of Vanilla

Vanilla beans were first picked from wild vines in the forest when they were ripe and already full of scent. Eventually, the Totonac farmed vanilla vines and learned how to cure the beans. At first, the Totonac used vanilla only for its scent, not its flavor, possibly using a few beans to scent their homes. In later years, it became a tradition for Totonac women to oil and braid the fragrant beans together, and wear them in their hair as a natural perfume.

(above) Vanilla pods, animal skins, and other supplies were traded between different peoples throughout Mesoamerica.

(below) Spices were used to ease pain and cure the sick. Vanilla was often used to treat stomach pain.

For the Love of Chocolatl

The Aztecs were Native Mesoamericans from the north of Mexico who rose to power between 1100 A.D. and 1500 A.D. They moved south into the Central Valley of Mexico and established a large capital city, Tenochtitlan, on the site of present-day Mexico City. They took over lands throughout present-day Mexico and made many other Native groups give them valuable trade items. Since vanilla did not grow near Tenochtitlan, the Aztecs demanded it from the Totonac. The Aztecs added vanilla to a drink they called chocolatl, which included cacao beans, corn, honey, and chili peppers.

Conquering Vanilla

Spices from Asia, such as pepper, were in great demand in Europe during the 1400s and 1500s and **expeditions** were sent to bring them back. When European explorers sailed westward, hoping to find a quicker route to Asia, they discovered the New World, which included North, South, and Central America. While the explorers did not find the spices they were looking for, they found other valuable plants and plant products, including vanilla.

Cinnamon and nutmeg were other spices from Asia that were prized by Europeans.

Welcoming an Army

Spain and other European countries were eager to expand their territories and lay claim to the riches and resources of the New World. In 1519, Hernando Cortés, a conquistador, set out from a Spanish settlement in Cuba seeking gold and glory in Mexico. He landed in what is now Veracruz, Mexico. With an army of 500 men, Cortés set out for Tenochtitlan, the capital city of the Aztec empire. When they reached the capital, the Spanish were greeted with great hospitality, or friendliness, by the Aztec leader, Montezuma II, who threw a large feast in their honor. At the feast, the Spanish were served chocolatl, which the Aztec believed was good for a person's health and gave them energy.

Many Mesoamerican groups wanted to be free of Montezuma's rule. Some groups helped Cortés later conquer the Aztec.

Cortés the Killer

In spite of this friendly beginning, relations between the Aztecs and the Spanish soon became hostile. Cortés, whose goal was to take over Aztec lands, kidnapped Montezuma and threatened to kill the leader if the Aztec people did not surrender their lands. The Aztecs revolted, or fought back, but their bows and arrows, wooden swords, and shields were no match for the cannon, guns, and armor of Cortés and his men. The Spanish eventually defeated the Aztec and conquered, or took over, all of Mexico. These lands, along with other areas, including parts of Central America and the Caribbean, became known as New Spain.

All Aztec men were trained to fight in wars but they were unable to defeat the well armed Spanish. Thousands of Aztecs were killed in the revolt.

The **colony** of New Spain offered many resources and plant products that were valued in Europe. Vanilla beans and other foods were shipped back to Spain in the early 1500s, along with silver and other metals that were mined in the colony.

The Flavors of New Spain

Chocolatl first became popular among the wealthy colonists of New Spain, including explorers and landowners. At first, these Europeans did not like the taste of chocolatl, as it was bitter and spicy, but they drank it because they believed it would make them healthy. In order to improve its taste, the women of New Spain served it hot instead of cold, and replaced some of the traditional ingredients with additions of their own, such as cinnamon and cane sugar. Only two ingredients were not changed: cacao beans and vanilla.

After 100 years of Spanish rule, the Native population went from about 20 million to about only one million. Many Native peoples died from diseases brought over by Europeans, including smallpox.

◀ *The Spanish named the bean* **vainilla**, *which comes from a Spanish word for "sheath," since the cured pod looks like a miniature sword sheath, or cover, shown at left.*

Vanilla in Europe

Shipments of goods were sent to Spain in large convoys, or groups of ships. The ships traveled together to guard against **pirates**. Vanilla and cacao beans from the shipments were used to prepare chocolatl. The drink became very popular, but because the ingredients were expensive, only royalty and members of the upper **class** in Spain could afford it. In the early 1600s, vanilla made its way from Spain to France, England, Italy, and other countries in Europe, usually as an ingredient in chocolate drinks. The flavor of vanilla became most popular in France where, by the mid-1700s, French chefs began to include vanilla in ice cream, pastries, and other treats, while it also may have been used as a scent in perfumes.

▲ *The term "French vanilla" is not a type of vanilla plant. It refers to a mixture of cream, sugar, vanilla bean, and egg yolk commonly used in France to make custard.*

Controlling a Spice

During the 1500s, Europe's supply of vanilla, cacao beans, and sugar came entirely from Spanish colonies, which allowed Spanish traders to charge high prices. Spain had conquered lands in Mexico, Central America, and the Caribbean. They fought to keep other countries from settling in these areas because they wanted to stay in control of supplies of vanilla and other valuable items, such as silver. It was not until the 1600s that France, the Netherlands, and England began to establish colonies in these areas. By the mid-1700s, all these countries had access to vanilla and Spain no longer controlled the vanilla supply.

Queen Elizabeth I of England's apothecary, a person who made medicines, introduced her to the flavor of vanilla. She loved the taste and became a devoted fan of vanilla pudding.

Vanilla Colonies

European countries also set up colonies on tropical islands in the Indian Ocean. Plantations were built on these islands that grew crops that could not be grown in the temperate, or mild, climates common to most of Europe. It was on one of these islands, Réunion, where the worldwide vanilla industry was born.

Réunion, an island near the east coast of Africa, used to be called Bourbon Island, after the French royal family that ruled at the time. Today, Réunion is still governed by France. The top quality vanilla produced in Réunion, as well as beans grown in Madagascar and other Indian Ocean islands, is called Bourbon vanilla.

Vanilla's Curse

Europeans had been trying to grow vanilla vines in greenhouses in Europe since the 1500s. While many were successful at growing the plant, no one was able to pollinate the vanilla orchid, which meant that beans were not produced. This was sometimes referred to as "the curse of Montezuma" because it was believed that the Aztec leader cursed the plant so that Europeans could not profit from it. The French brought vanilla plants to Réunion, one of their colonies in the Indian Ocean. They hoped that because the environment and weather were similar to conditions in Mexico, the plants would grow and produce beans.

Réunion

Réunion is a small island that lies east of Madagascar in the Indian Ocean. The warm, humid climate and rich volcanic soil of the island make it an ideal place to grow crops that need a tropical climate. During the 1700s, coffee and sugar plantations were set up by wealthy French colonists. Slaves were brought to the island from Madagascar and East Africa to work on the plantations. Vanilla cuttings, or pieces of vanilla vines that could be planted to grow a new vine, were first brought to Réunion in 1819 but these vines died after several months. In 1822, new cuttings arrived. These cuttings grew into vines but did not produce beans. No one understood why the beans would not grow.

A Boy Named Edmond

A 12-year-old slave named Edmond Albius discovered the trick to pollinating vanilla. Albius was a house slave on a plantation in Réunion belonging to Ferreol Bellier-Beaumont, a French colonist who had been growing vanilla vines as a hobby for 20 years. His vines had never produced beans. One day in 1841 he found two beans growing on one of his vines. Albius had learned about orchids from Bellier-Beaumont, and he experimented on his own to find a way to pollinate the plants.

Réunion was wild and uninhabited when first discovered by the French. French planters brought thousands of slaves to the island.

Making a Bean

When it was discovered that vanilla orchids were not being pollinated anywhere but in Mexico and Central America, botonists, or plant scientists, tried to pollinate vanilla by hand but were unsuccessful in finding a quick and easy method. In order for pollination to occur, pollen, which is stored in the anther, must come in contact with a part of the flower called the stigma. In a vanilla orchid, the pollen is covered by a flap of tissue called the rostellum. Edmond Albius used a small pointed piece of bamboo to peel back the rostellum. This exposed the pollen, which he then smeared on the stigma. When the pollen contacts the stigma, a long pollen tube grows down into the flower. Once the pollen tube touches the ovary, or egg cell, at the base of the flower, pollination occurs and the ovary develops into a vanilla bean.

The Birth of an Industry

Plantation owners in Réunion were quick to put Albius' technique to use, and soon vanilla was the island's main crop. News traveled fast throughout other European colonies, and over the next several decades, vanilla plantations thrived in the nearby islands of Mauritius, the Seychelles, and Madagascar, as well as islands further east such as Indonesia and Tahiti. By the 1880s, vanilla production in these regions was greater than it was in Mexico, which had been, up to that point, the main supplier of vanilla.

anther (pollen)

rostellum

stigma

petal

A Bee's Business

Before vanilla orchids were pollinated by hand, beans were only produced in Mexico and Central America, the places where vanilla vines grew wild. This was because only a certain kind of bee that was native to these areas pollinated vanilla orchids. The bees crawled into the flowers looking for nectar, or food. Pollen stuck to their backs and brushed off against the stigma of the next flowers the bees landed on, resulting in the pollination of the vanilla orchid.

▸ *This illustration is of a cross section of a vanilla orchid. A cross section shows what an object looks like if it was cut in half, revealing the parts inside.*

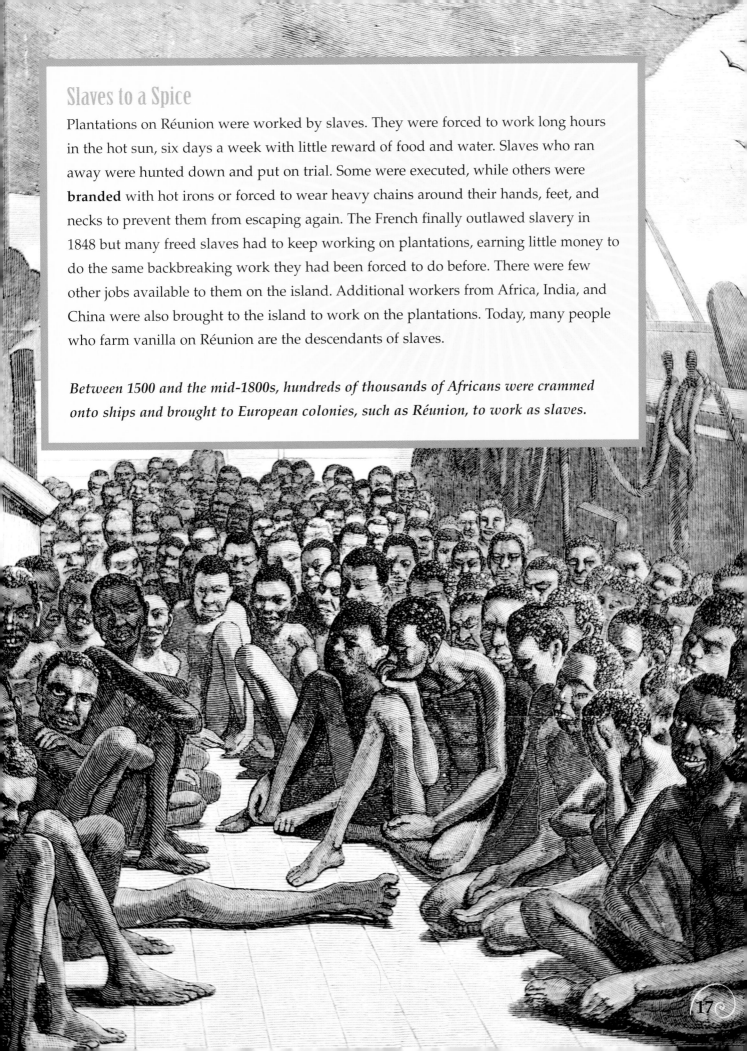

Slaves to a Spice

Plantations on Réunion were worked by slaves. They were forced to work long hours in the hot sun, six days a week with little reward of food and water. Slaves who ran away were hunted down and put on trial. Some were executed, while others were **branded** with hot irons or forced to wear heavy chains around their hands, feet, and necks to prevent them from escaping again. The French finally outlawed slavery in 1848 but many freed slaves had to keep working on plantations, earning little money to do the same backbreaking work they had been forced to do before. There were few other jobs available to them on the island. Additional workers from Africa, India, and China were also brought to the island to work on the plantations. Today, many people who farm vanilla on Réunion are the descendants of slaves.

Between 1500 and the mid-1800s, hundreds of thousands of Africans were crammed onto ships and brought to European colonies, such as Réunion, to work as slaves.

Growing Vanilla

Vanilla is one of the most labor-intensive crops to grow, which means it requires a lot of time and work to grow, harvest, cure, and dry the beans. Farmers must watch the crops carefully, knowing exactly when to prune the vines, pollinate the orchids, and pick the beans. Many farmers continue to grow vanilla because it brings in more money per pound than other crops, such as rice or **sugar cane**, which are often grown in the same regions as vanilla.

A worker pollinates an orchid. The vine is growing on another tree. In the wild, vanilla vines are epiphytes, or plants that live on other plants but do not harm them.

Wild Vanilla

Vanilla vines first grew wild in the forests of Mesoamerica where they grew from seeds. Seed pods, or vanilla beans, carry thousands of seeds. In the wild, when a bean ripens on the vine it eventually splits open to release the seeds inside. The seeds fall to the ground and get covered by soil, or eaten by an animal, who will then deposit the seed in its droppings in a new location. They may also be blown to new areas by the wind. Once the seed lands in soil, it must be infected by a certain kind of **fungus** that is found in the soil. The fungus gives it the nutrients it needs to grow into a healthy vine.

Cultivating Vanilla

The first step in growing vines on farms or plantations is to provide them with tutors, or support structures that they can grow on. Vanilla vines are epiphytes, which means in the wild they grow on other plants. Concrete, metal, or wooden posts are sometimes used for this purpose on farms but it is most common to use trees or bushes. Vanilla cuttings are planted alongside the tutors and climb up the tutors' trunks and branches. Tutors are usually planted one year before the vines to give them a head start on growing. It takes up to three years before vanilla flowers bloom.

Handling an Orchid

Flowering occurs over a two-month period in early spring. Workers must watch the vines carefully because each flower is only in bloom for six to eight hours from early morning to early afternoon. Each flower is pollinated by hand. Experienced workers can pollinate up to 1,000 orchids in a single day, using bamboo splinters, toothpicks, leaf stems, or their own fingernails to uncover the pollen and transfer it to the stigma.

▲ *Plantations use vanilla cuttings to grow new vines. A cutting is a piece of a vine that has been cut from another plant and is placed in soil. It sprouts new roots, resulting in a new vine.*

◄ *Orchids are often pollinated by women rather than men. Their smaller fingers make it easier to handle the delicate parts of the flower.*

19

Fermentation and curing, or drying, brings out the flavor and aroma of the vanilla, while at the same time preparing the beans for sale or storage. Drying the beans helps prevent them from rotting.

Harvesting

Vanilla beans appear about six weeks after an orchid is pollinated, and spend the next six to nine months growing on the vine. Most beans are picked when they are green with a slightly yellowish tip. If beans are picked too early, they will be poor quality because they will not yet contain enough vanillin and other chemicals which develop into the rich vanilla flavor and scent. If the beans are left too long on the vine, they split open, and are worth less because of their flawed appearance.

Curing

After the beans are picked, they are "killed," often by dipping them in hot water, which stops the bean from growing and fermenting. At this stage the beans turn from green to dark brown. For four to six weeks, the beans are laid out in the sun during the day and placed in cloth-lined boxes to "sweat," or release moisture, at night. Their color becomes a deeper brown. The beans are then spread out in the shade for two to three months to dry further. Dried beans are placed in airtight boxes for three more months to strengthen their flavor and scent.

Sorting

Vanilla beans are sorted into different grades, or categories, according to length, girth, or fatness, color, aroma, oiliness of the skin, and whether or not the skin has splits or marks. Grading systems vary from region to region, but generally, beans are divided into top, standard, and low grade. Top grade beans are straight, thick, at least eight inches (20 centimeters) long, with a shiny dark brown color, and an oily surface. They have soft, smooth skin unmarked by splits or spots and often have white powder on their surface, which are crystals of vanillin. Lower grade beans usually have a lot of flavor and aroma but may be curved, with splits or marks on the skin. Once the beans are sorted, they are ready to be sold.

Workers sort beans into different grades. Some top quality beans are sold to gourmet restaurants, while lower grades are often used in vanilla extracts.

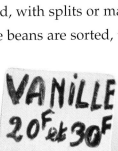

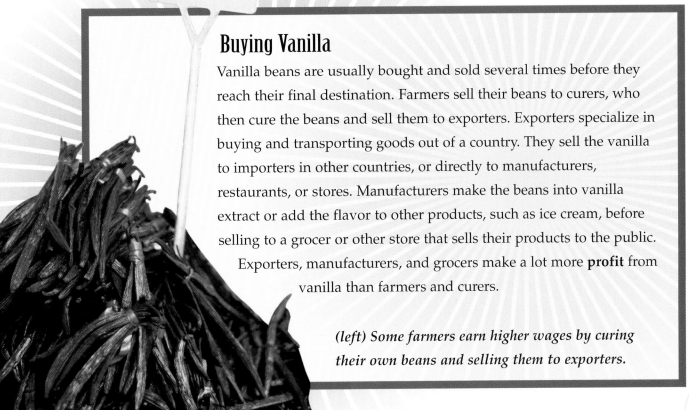

Buying Vanilla

Vanilla beans are usually bought and sold several times before they reach their final destination. Farmers sell their beans to curers, who then cure the beans and sell them to exporters. Exporters specialize in buying and transporting goods out of a country. They sell the vanilla to importers in other countries, or directly to manufacturers, restaurants, or stores. Manufacturers make the beans into vanilla extract or add the flavor to other products, such as ice cream, before selling to a grocer or other store that sells their products to the public. Exporters, manufacturers, and grocers make a lot more **profit** from vanilla than farmers and curers.

(left) Some farmers earn higher wages by curing their own beans and selling them to exporters.

Green Gold

The largest supplier of raw vanilla in the world today is Madagascar, an island country off the southeastern coast of Africa. Vanilla is one of Madagascar's most valuable crops, providing money for many people, including farmers. Some Malagasy, or people from Madagascar, call vanilla "green gold."

Security Measures

Theft is always a problem for vanilla farmers and curers, especially when vanilla prices are high. Some farmers pick their beans early to prevent them from being stolen from the vines, which results in lower quality beans. Farmers and managers of curing plants sleep near their crops or store of beans, armed with guns to stop thieves from stealing vanilla beans. Many curing houses search their workers at the end of each day. A few pounds of vanilla may be worth more than a worker makes in a year, and curing houses do not want beans to be stolen.

Vanilla farmers often "tattoo" their beans, stamping a mark into them while they are still on the vine. Each farm has its own mark. Anyone trying to sell beans that have a mark belonging to another farm is arrested.

The History of Vanilla in Madagascar

Cuttings from vanilla vines were first brought to Madagascar in 1840 on French ships and planted in the rainforests along the northeastern coast. It was not until 1870 that Edmond Albius' technique of hand pollination reached Madagascar. The island became a French colony in 1895, and wealthy French colonists hired the Malagasy people to work on plantations. France gave up control of Madagascar in 1960, and now 90 percent of vanilla is grown by families in the SAVA region, an area along the northeast coast. Today, groups such as the GNEV (*Groupement National des Exportateurs de Vanille de Madagascar*) help ensure that Madagascar grows and exports only the finest beans.

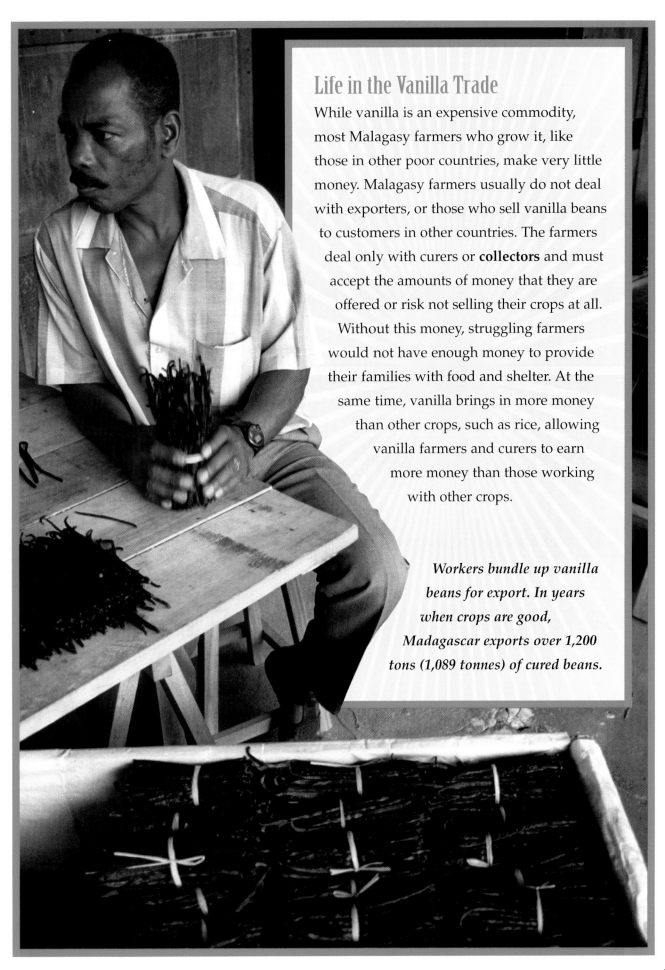

Life in the Vanilla Trade

While vanilla is an expensive commodity, most Malagasy farmers who grow it, like those in other poor countries, make very little money. Malagasy farmers usually do not deal with exporters, or those who sell vanilla beans to customers in other countries. The farmers deal only with curers or **collectors** and must accept the amounts of money that they are offered or risk not selling their crops at all. Without this money, struggling farmers would not have enough money to provide their families with food and shelter. At the same time, vanilla brings in more money than other crops, such as rice, allowing vanilla farmers and curers to earn more money than those working with other crops.

Workers bundle up vanilla beans for export. In years when crops are good, Madagascar exports over 1,200 tons (1,089 tonnes) of cured beans.

Vanilla Tahitensis

Tahiti is part of French Polynesia, a group of tropical islands located in the Pacific Ocean, halfway between Australia and South America. The islands of Tahiti are home to a species of vanilla grown in very few places in the world. While only 4.4 to 5.5 tons (four to five tonnes) of Tahitian vanilla is exported every year, there is a high demand for the beans because of their distinctive flavor and scent.

Europeans had a great influence on Tahitian life. This picture from 1880 shows Tahitan women wearing traditional and European clothing.

The History of Vanilla Tahitensis

During the 1700s, Spanish botanists produced a new kind of vanilla by **crossbreeding** two different species of wild vanilla vines that had come from Mesoamerica. This new variety of vanilla was brought to Tahiti, a **protectorate** of France, by a French ship commander, Admiral Ferdinand-Alphonse Hamelin, in 1848. Hamelin presented the new variety to the Tahitian governor as a gift. Some people believe that these vanilla vines were then crossbred with others brought to Tahiti in later years to produce the new species *Vanilla tahitensis*.

A Different Breed

Tahitian vanilla is known for its floral scent and fruity taste, which contains a hint of licorice and cherry flavor. While Tahitian vanilla is low in vanillin, the chemical compound that gives Bourbon and Mexican vanilla much of its taste, it is high in other compounds, such as heliotropin, a chemical often used to scent soaps and perfumes. Tahitian vanilla vines have flowers that are creamy-white in color. Most beans are only four to five inches (ten to 13 centimeters) long, fat, and have a thick outer skin.

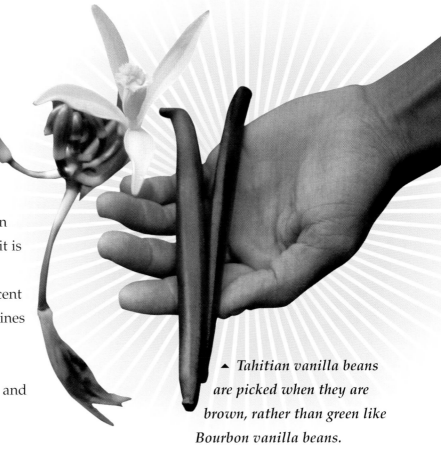

▲ *Tahitian vanilla beans are picked when they are brown, rather than green like Bourbon vanilla beans.*

The Start of an Industry

Large-scale farming of vanilla began in Tahiti in the late 1800s. French **missionaries** who had come to Tahiti to **convert** the Tahitians to **Catholicism**, the main religion in France, had learned how to grow and cure vanilla beans while on French colonies in the Indian Ocean. They passed on what they learned to Native Tahitians who worked on French plantations. Up until the mid-1900s, Bourbon vanilla was the most popular type of vanilla, but many manufacturers began using Tahitian vanilla because it was cheaper. Eventually, the taste of Tahitian beans caught on, especially with gourmet chefs and perfumeries. Today, Tahitian vanilla is the most expensive type in the world.

Today, many tourists in Tahiti enjoy learning about the rich Tahitian culture. Hotels and other tourist sites have taken over areas once used by Tahitian vanilla farmers.

A Great Decline

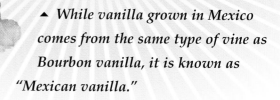

During the 1700s and early 1800s, Mexico was the center of the vanilla industry, producing the majority of vanilla. Once plantations were established in other parts of the world, and cheap artificial extracts became available, Mexican exporters were selling fewer beans. Today, Mexico sells less than five percent of all vanilla.

▲ *While vanilla grown in Mexico comes from the same type of vine as Bourbon vanilla, it is known as "Mexican vanilla."*

The City that Perfumed the World

The city of Papantla, in the state of Veracruz, was established by the Totonac peoples and is where the vanilla trade began. Beginning in the 1700s, Totonac farmers from the surrounding area brought vanilla beans picked from the forests into Papantla to be cured and sold. The beans were laid out on rooftops, streets, and patios to dry in the sun. The beans could be smelled up to five miles (eight kilometers) away. Papantla was known for producing top quality vanilla and was called "the city that perfumed the world." By the early 1900s, oil companies had come to Mexico to drill for oil. They destroyed a lot of land, forcing many farmers to give up growing vanilla and other crops.

Many farmers from Papantla took jobs with oil companies in the early 1900s. Lands in Veracruz, including farms, were destroyed when oil wells were set up and also when oil fires broke out.

Vanilla Farming

Today, vanilla in Mexico is grown mostly on small farms by *campesinos*. *Campesinos* are local Mexican farmers who live outside the main towns throughout Mexico. In small villages outside of Veracruz, one farmer is often chosen to take all of the vanilla beans to the nearest town to be sold. They, like farmers in Madagascar, often do not know how much vanilla is sold for on the **global market** and must accept the prices offered by the *beneficiadores*, or those who cure, package, and sell the beans for export. The *campesinos* make little money, often struggling to support themselves and their families.

A Bad Rap

A few dishonest vanilla manufacturers in Mexico have contributed to the decline in vanilla sales. Some extracts made in Mexico, labeled as natural vanilla extract, turned out to be artificial extract. In order to make these imitation extracts taste and smell like natural vanilla, some manufacturers added coumarin, a chemical naturally found in tonka beans and other plants. Coumarin was banned in the United States by the Food and Drug Administration in the 1950s because it causes liver damage, and possibly cancer. Rules in Mexico that state what must be written on product labels are less strict than those in the rest of North America, and coumarin may still be found in some Mexican extracts.

Mexican revolutionary leader Emiliano Zapata is a hero to many Mexican campesinos, or farming peasants. During the Mexican Revolution (1910-1920), Zapata fought the government, who had seized peasant land and given it to wealthy landowners. Most vanilla is still grown by campesinos on small plots of land.

Flavoring the World

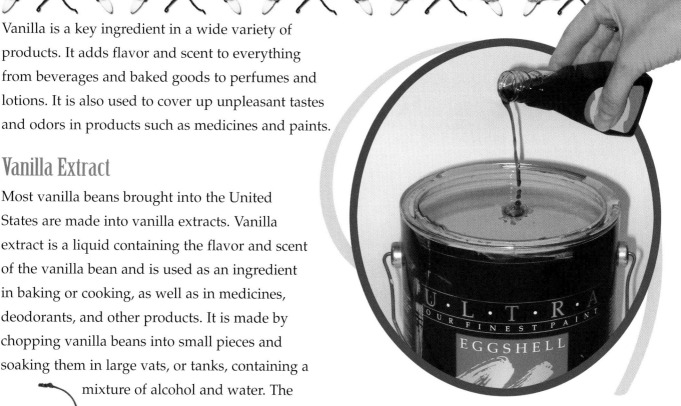

Vanilla is a key ingredient in a wide variety of products. It adds flavor and scent to everything from beverages and baked goods to perfumes and lotions. It is also used to cover up unpleasant tastes and odors in products such as medicines and paints.

Vanilla Extract

Most vanilla beans brought into the United States are made into vanilla extracts. Vanilla extract is a liquid containing the flavor and scent of the vanilla bean and is used as an ingredient in baking or cooking, as well as in medicines, deodorants, and other products. It is made by chopping vanilla beans into small pieces and soaking them in large vats, or tanks, containing a mixture of alcohol and water. The pieces of beans remain in the vats for about one week. Some manufacturers also heat the mixture. The extract is then filtered and bottled. Sugar, corn syrup, or other additives are often added to extracts to give a sweet aftertaste, but the highest quality extracts contain few additives.

A Fold of Vanilla

The vanilla extract sold in grocery stores is sometimes called "single-fold" extract. It contains 13.5 ounces (383 grams) of beans per gallon (four liters) of liquid, which is a mixture of alcohol and water. Double-fold, three-fold, and four-fold extracts are more concentrated, or stronger, containing two, three, or four times as many vanilla beans as single-fold extract.

▲ *People painting their homes can add a few tablespoons of vanilla to the paint to mask the unpleasant smell.*

◄ *Stronger extracts, such as double-fold or three-fold, are used to make vanilla flavored products, such as ice cream, cookies, and candy.*

28

▶ Artificial Extract

Artificial extracts are cheaper than real vanilla extracts and lack the true vanilla taste. They contain vanillin, the main flavor ingredient found in natural vanilla, but it is cheaply produced from other sources, such as pine sap and clove oil, as well as from lignin, a waste product of paper manufacturing.

A Dusting of Vanilla

Ground vanilla is dried vanilla beans ground to a fine powder. It has a strong flavor, giving baked goods a rich vanilla taste.

▶ Bean There

Whole vanilla beans are used in cooking and baking, and often left to soak in liquids such as custards and creams, giving them a rich vanilla flavor. Gourmet chefs also use vanilla beans to decorate meals. They buy high quality beans with no marks or splits.

◀ Absolutely Vanilla

"Vanilla absolute" is the most concentrated extract available. Due to its high price, it is used only in the finest, most expensive perfumes.

We All Scream for Ice Cream

Thomas Jefferson, president of the United States from 1801 to 1809, introduced vanilla to the American colonies in the late 1700s. While spending four years in France as a **diplomat**, he came across a delicacy called vanilla ice cream. When Jefferson returned to his home in Philadelphia, Pennsylvania, he found that ice cream was becoming popular among the wealthy but he could not find vanilla ice cream. He had a friend in Paris send him 50 vanilla beans, making Jefferson the first to bring vanilla to the United States.

Threatening a Bean

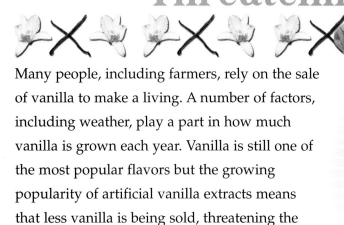

Many people, including farmers, rely on the sale of vanilla to make a living. A number of factors, including weather, play a part in how much vanilla is grown each year. Vanilla is still one of the most popular flavors but the growing popularity of artificial vanilla extracts means that less vanilla is being sold, threatening the livelihood of many vanilla farmers and workers.

Tropical Storms

While tropical zones provide an ideal climate for vanilla vines, they are also the areas worst hit by hurricanes, cyclones, and floods. Tropical storms bring strong winds and heavy rains that tear flowers and fruit from the vines or uproot plants. In 2000, Cyclone Hudah tore through northeastern Madagascar with winds nearing 200 miles per hour (322 kilometers per hour). Floods and landslides destroyed 35 percent of the country's vanilla crop.

(above) Vanilla vines can be infected by disease, such as vanilla mosaic virus, that can weaken or even kill a farmer's vanilla crop. Vanilla vines are infected if vines are pruned with tools already used on diseased vines or through insects that feed on the plants.

(below) Widespread flooding was caused by a tropical storm that hit Mexico in 1999. The state of Veracruz was hit hard, and much of Mexico's vanilla crop was wiped out.

Stormy Prices

At the time of Cyclone Hudah, Madagascar supplied about 80 percent of the world's vanilla. The heavy losses to its crops, so soon after a lot of Mexico's crops were also destroyed in a storm, created a worldwide vanilla shortage. Between 1999 and 2003, prices soared, in some cases increasing from $20 per pound (0.5 kilogram) to over $225 per pound. Countries such as Uganda, Tonga, India, and Costa Rica, which had never been big vanilla producers, planted more vanilla to keep up with the demand. At the time, many companies that used vanilla in their products also switched to cheaper artificial extracts. When crops in storm-hit areas recovered, there was too much vanilla available, causing prices to fall sharply.

The Quest for Fair Trade

Fair Trade is a worldwide program that helps workers on small farms in many countries throughout Africa, Asia, and Latin America earn a wage that is enough to cover basic living expenses, such as food and shelter. Fair Trade farmers follow rules set out by the program. For example, they must produce high-quality crops using practices that are environmentally friendly, such as avoiding the use of **herbicides** and **pesticides** that are dangerous. Exporters, importers, and supermarkets all play a part in supporting Fair Trade by choosing to buy products from Fair Trade-certified producers. Fair Trade vanilla has become available in many parts of the world. When more people become interested in purchasing Fair Trade products, more stores and importers will offer Fair Trade vanilla to their customers.

Over 98 percent of the vanilla flavor in food products comes from artificial extracts. Many people in vanilla growing areas lost their jobs when artificial vanilla became popular.

31

Glossary

brand To put a permanent mark on something

cacao beans Beans used to make chocolate

Catholicism The religion of the Roman Catholic Church, an organization headed by the Pope

chemical compound A substance that makes up a solid, liquid, or gas, and is itself made up of two or more simpler substances

class A group of people in a society who share similar amounts of wealth

collector A person who gathers vanilla beans from farms and brings them to curers

colony Territory that is ruled by another country

conquistador A Spanish explorer who conquered new lands for Spain

convert To change one's religion, faith, or beliefs

crossbreed Producing a plant by mating, or bringing together, two different types of plants

cure To preserve and prepare a product before it is sold or used

developing country A country that does not have a lot of industry or wealth

diplomat A country's representative

expedition A voyage taken with a specific goal, such as finding new land

extract Flavored liquid used in cooking or baking

ferment To begin to break down or rot

fungus A group of plant-like organisms that live in soil, such as molds and mushrooms

global market All the countries in the world that trade with each other

herbicide Chemicals used to kill weeds

incense A substance burned to release a scent

Mesoamerican Native peoples who lived in central or southern Mexico, and parts of Central America, before Europeans arrived

missionary Someone who goes to another country to spread their religion

pesticide Chemicals used to kill insects

pirate A person who attacks and robs ships

pollinate The act of joining two parts of a plant together, eventually resulting in seeds

profit The amount of money earned from the sale of a product

protectorate A country that is protected and partially controlled by another country

revolutionary A person fighting to overthrow, or remove, the government

smallpox A disease that causes fever and puss-filled blisters to appear on the skin

sugar cane A type of grass used to make sugar

tropics The areas directly north and south of the equator

Index

Printed in the U.S.A.